AIR & SEA MYSTERIES

BY SUE HAMILTON

VISIT US AT
WWW.ABDOPUBLISHING.COM

Published by ABDO Publishing Company, 8000 West 78th Street, Suite 310, Edina, Minnesota 55439.

Printed in the United States.

Editor: John Hamilton
Graphic Design: Sue Hamilton
Cover Design: Neil Klinepier
Cover Illustration: Amelia Earhart, Getty Images
Interior Photos and Illustrations: p 4 Diver by propeller, iStockphoto; Nauticos Earhart Discovery logo, ©2001 Nauticos, LLC; p 5 Earhart collage, Getty Images; TIGHAR logo, courtesy The International Group for Historic Aviation Recovery; p 6 TIGHAR The Earhart Project logo, p 7 Earhart and Noonan, AP Images; pp 8-9 Earhart walking by plane, courtesy Smithsonian Institution; p 10 *Itasca*, courtesy United States Coast Guard; USS *Colorado*, courtesy U.S. Naval Historical Center; p 11 Amelia Earhart, AP Images; p 12 Nikumaroro, Corbis; Gillespie with plexiglass, AP Images; p 13 David Jourdan, courtesy Nauticos, LLC; Map of Nikumaroro area, Cartesia/Hamilton; p 14 Charles Nungesser, Getty Images; François Coli, courtesy *TIGHAR Tracks* September 1993; p 15 Nungesser and Coli, Getty Images; pp 16-17 The White Bird, Getty Images; p 18 Charles Lindbergh lands in France, AP Images; p 19 Newfoundland, iStockphoto; p 20 Map of the *White Bird*'s route, Cartesia/Hamilton; p 21 Lindbergh and Orteig, Wikimedia; Charles Nungesser, Getty Images; François Coli, Getty Images; p 22 Captain Benjamin Spooner Briggs, courtesy Find A Grave; The Marie Celeste stamp sheet, courtesy Maldives; p 23 *Amazon,* ©Parks Canada, Dartmouth, NS; p 25 Ship at sea, iStockphoto; p 26 USS *Cyclops*, courtesy U.S. Naval Historical Center; p 27 Fleet entering Rio de Janeiro, Corbis; p 28 German U-boat, Corbis; p 29 Earnest Crammer, courtesy U.S. Naval Historical Center; p 31 Amelia Earhart, Getty Images.

Library of Congress Cataloging-in-Publication Data

Hamilton, Sue L., 1959-
  Air & sea mysteries / Sue Hamilton.
    p. cm. -- (Unsolved mysteries)
  Includes index.
  ISBN 978-1-59928-837-6
  1. Aircraft accidents--Juvenile literature. 2. Aircraft accidents--Investigation--Juvenile literature. 3. Shipwrecks--Juvenile literature. I. Title. II. Title: Air and sea mysteries.

TL553.5.H36 2007
629.1309--dc22

2007014551

CONTENTS

AIR & SEA MYSTERIES

Above: A diver explores a shipwreck.

In our history books, there are many examples of fearless explorers who set off in their ships and planes, vanishing without a trace into the unknown. Some have called them brave, while others criticize them for being foolhardy. Others say they were simply unlucky. These sailors and fliers are remembered not just because of their skills and knowledge, but also because of their mysterious and tragic deaths. What happened to them?

Some doomed explorers left hints about their final fate: route and flight plans, static-filled or faded radio transmissions, warnings of violent weather encounters, odd compass readings. Some ships and planes have completely disappeared, becoming the most perplexing unsolved mysteries of our time.

Two of the most-researched historical mysteries involved experienced pilots and their navigators. In the summer of 1937, Amelia Earhart took to the skies, attempting to become the first woman to pilot a plane around the world. On July 2, 1937, she and her navigator, Fred Noonan, disappeared somewhere over the Pacific Ocean. Ten years earlier, in May 1927, French World War I heroes Charles Nungesser and François Coli took off from France, attempting to fly nonstop across the Atlantic Ocean to New York City. The men and their plane, the *White Bird*, vanished from the face of the earth. What happened to these experienced fliers?

In the centuries before modern communication devices, it was common for ships to disappear, never to be seen again. These were dangerous times, and friends and family knew that weather and fate could send the strongest ship and the most experienced sailors down to Davy Jones' Locker. However, wireless radiotelegraphy (known today simply as radio) changed all that. Invented around the turn of the 20th century, radio allowed travelers to send ship-to-ship or ship-to-shore distress messages. This saved many lives.

Below: Nauticos is a group of deep-water explorers who use state-of-the-art technology to uncover historical wrecks on the ocean floor.

Left: Amelia Earhart, one of the world's first female pilots, was lost forever on July 2, 1937.

However, even though communication devices improved throughout the years, ships and their crews continued to be lost at sea.

The fate of those lost ships haunts and fascinates us. Several organizations have been created to search for answers. The International Group for Historic Aviation Recovery (TIGHAR, pronounced "tiger") is an organization of aviation archaeologists seeking solutions to air mysteries. Nauticos is a scientific organization that uses advanced equipment at deep ocean depths to find long-lost shipwrecks. Although ships have been discovered, there remain many air and sea mysteries for which answers are waiting to be found.

Above: TIGHAR searches for missing pilots and planes, including the *White Bird*, lost in May 1927.

AMELIA EARHART & FRED NOONAN

Pilot Amelia Earhart broke speed and altitude records in the 1920s and 1930s. In 1928, she was the first woman to fly across the Atlantic Ocean. Four years later, she became the first woman to fly alone across that same great ocean. She received the Distinguished Flying Cross from the U.S. Congress, the National Geographic Society's Gold Medal from President Herbert Hoover, and the French government's Cross of Knight of the Legion of Honor. She wrote books, spoke to countless audiences, and helped start an airline and a flight school. She became known as the "First Lady of the Air."

In 1937, Earhart attempted to become the first woman to fly around the world at the equator, the earth's widest point. However, unlike her other challenges, she did not succeed at this one. Earhart and her navigator, Fred Noonan, disappeared on July 2, 1937.

A month earlier, Amelia Earhart took off from Miami, Florida, on June 1, 1937, in her Lockheed 10E Electra plane on what was called her "World Flight." The only other person aboard was Noonan, a former commercial pilot. They had started their journey flying cross-country from Oakland, California. Now, as they continued their eastward trip around the world, they refueled the plane at locations in South America, Africa, Asia, and Australia. On June 29, they arrived in Lae, New Guinea, just north of Australia. They had only 7,000 miles (11,265 km) left of their 29,000-mile (46,671-km) journey, but there was still much danger. Not only would they have a 20-hour trip ahead of them, they'd be flying over the Pacific Ocean, the world's largest body of water. Finding their way, with very few landmarks to guide them, would be extremely difficult.

Above: Famous aviator Amelia Earhart and her navigator Fred Noonan stand before their twin-engine Lockheed Electra in Los Angeles, California, in May 1937, prior to their attempt to fly around the world.

Earhart and Noonan were headed for Howland Island, a tiny piece of land 2,556 miles (4,113 km) northeast of Lae. This 1.5-mile (2.4-k) -long speck of coral was a convenient halfway point between New Guinea and their next destination, Hawaii. Howland Island had a landing field that had been built just a few months earlier. The Lockheed Electra would be refueled by the United States Coast Guard Cutter *Itasca*, which was stationed in the area and waiting for them.

Full of optimism, Earhart and Noonan set off on the longest leg of their journey at 12:30 p.m. on July 2, 1937. They would cross the International Date Line, so the date they took off from Lae and the date they arrived at Howland Island would be the same. The Electra plane was equipped with more than enough fuel, plus the U.S. Navy ship USS *Ontario* was waiting midway between New Guinea and Howland Island to receive messages and act as a navigation beacon. In these days before satellite tracking technology, Noonan would be plotting their flight using the sun and stars, and depending on radio contact to assist them.

However, the USS *Ontario* received no radio transmissions from Earhart's plane. *Itasca* began receiving transmissions from Earhart 14 hours after the flight left Lae.

Above: Amelia Earhart stands by her Lockheed Electra.

Radio operators tried to call back, but no two-way communication was ever established with Earhart, whose call-letter identification was KHAQQ. Crewmen tried to find the plane based on the radio transmission. This also failed. Thick, black smoke was sent up as a location signal for the fliers. At 7:42 a.m. on July 2, 1937, Earhart radioed:

"KHAQQ calling Itasca. *We must be on you but cannot see you. But gas is running low. Been unable to reach you by radio. We are flying at 1,000 feet."*

The captain and crew of the *Itasca* were worried. Commander Warner Thompson kept his radio operators on the air, desperately trying to contact Earhart. Two more radio messages were received by the *Itasca*, until finally, at 8:43 a.m., Earhart's last official message was heard, with an approximate location and radio frequency:

"KHAQQ to Itasca *we are on the line 157 337 will repeat message we will repeat this on 6210 KCS wait…"*

Above: When Earhart's transmissions ended on July 2, 1937, the Coast Guard cutter *Itasca* began an immediate search.

Above: The battleship USS *Colorado* arrived in the area to help with one of the biggest search-and-rescue missions ever. Earhart was never found.

Twenty hours and 13 minutes after leaving New Guinea, Earhart and Noonan were heard no more. The fate of the two aviators would become an ongoing unsolved mystery.

One of the biggest search-and-rescue missions ever undertaken began within hours of Earhart's last radio transmission. The *Itasca* began searching immediately. Shortly thereafter, the battleship USS *Colorado* steamed to the area, sending up pilots in floatplanes to search for the popular flier. The aircraft carrier USS *Lexington* joined the search. Japan's *Koshu,* an oceanographic survey ship in the area, looked for the lost pilots. When radio signals were heard on frequencies that Earhart had been using, the world grew hopeful that the aviators were alive and would soon be found.

But the days turned into weeks. Finally, on July 18, 1937, the search was officially called off. Most believed the Electra had encountered heavy headwinds, causing Earhart to use up her fuel. Unable to receive a radio signal or find Howland Island, Earhart had run out of gas. Some believe the plane ditched in the water, sinking away into the vastness of the Pacific Ocean. Others guessed that Earhart and Noonan landed on a deserted island. Perhaps they were hurt and lived for a short while, which might explain the radio signals that searchers had heard. Or perhaps the two fliers were unhurt, but their radio was broken. Unable to contact anyone, they eventually died in some remote location.

But other people disagree. Ideas range from the farfetched to the possible. Some suggest that aliens captured the pilots and their plane. Others believe that Earhart and Noonan lived out their lives under new, secret identities. Still others think that the two fliers were captured and held by the Japanese as spies, dying in prison. (Japan's government has always denied this.)

What really happened to Amelia Earhart and Fred Noonan? The search has gone on for over 70 years. TIGHAR (The International Group for Historic Aviation Recovery) has scientifically searched every lead possible, centering their efforts on the tiny island of Nikumaroro (once called Gardner Island). Based on Earhart's last reported position, Nikumaroro lies directly in line with the flight plan. Only 400 miles (644 km) south of Howland Island and surrounded by thousands of miles of open ocean, Nikumaroro is one of the few places where Earhart could have attempted a landing.

Above: Amelia Earhart was a skilled pilot. Some believe she could have landed her plane on an island. However, others believe that the plane went down in the Pacific Ocean.

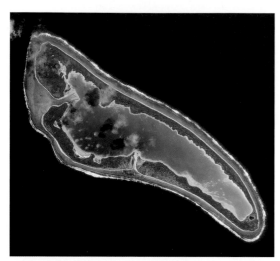

Above: A satellite image of Nikumaroro, an island in the Pacific Ocean where Amelia Earhart may have attempted to land her plane. The blue color is a lagoon in the center of the island.

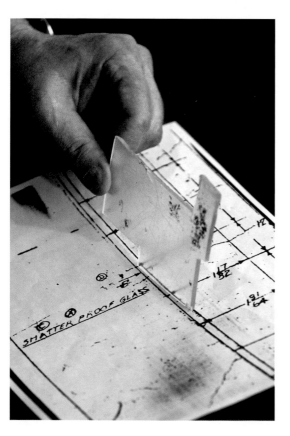

TIGHAR has found a number of artifacts on the island that could have come from Earhart's plane, including pieces of aluminum, plexi-type glass, and the remains of a woman's shoe, the size and style of which could have been worn by Amelia Earhart. TIGHAR has researched clues and interviewed many people—native islanders, military personnel, and anyone or their family members who once lived on Nikumaroro. Because the island was only inhabited from late 1938 until 1963, few people remain who have ever been on Nikumaroro.

TIGHAR has also thoroughly researched the historical paperwork on human bones that were found on the island in 1940. It was believed that the partial skeleton might have been Amelia Earhart's, although the physician who examined the bones at the time did not think so. However, in reviewing the doctor's detailed notes, a modern forensic anthropologist believes otherwise. A forensic anthropologist is someone who uses scientific methods to identify skeletal remains. Unfortunately, the actual bones have been lost. The search for the bones, which might provide the ultimate proof of Earhart's last days, continues.

Left: In February 2007, Ric Gillespie, executive director of TIGHAR, displayed a piece of plexi-type glass against original engineering drawings for the windows of the Lockheed Electra flown by Amelia Earhart. He recovered the item from a search site on Nikumaroro.

While TIGHAR searched for answers on land, another company, Nauticos Corporation, began a deep-sea search for Earhart's Lockheed 10E Electra plane in 2002. Founder and marine explorer David Jourdan says that the near-freezing water temperatures on the ocean floor are perfect for preserving lost aircraft. Using sonar, he is searching a 1,000-square-nautical mile (3,430-square-kilometer) area of the Pacific Ocean near Howland Island, Amelia Earhart's ultimate destination. This is a huge area, and the work is frustrating and sometimes difficult. Far from civilization, health issues of the crew, as well as equipment problems, have hindered Nauticos' work in the past, but Jourdan is determined to continue exploring.

Both Nauticos and TIGHAR are continuing their searches, each hoping for the ultimate discovery and a final answer to the unsolved mystery of the First Lady of the Air.

Above: Nauticos' David Jourdan is searching an area of the Pacific Ocean where he believes wreckage still remains of Earhart's Lockheed Electra. *Below:* Earhart never reached Howland.

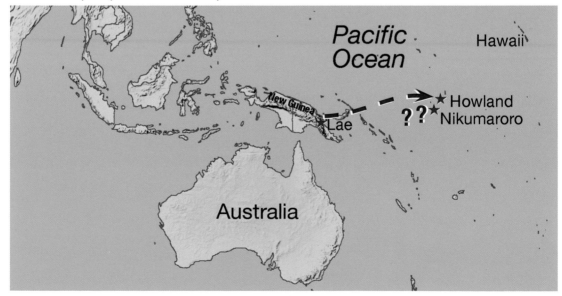

Above: French pilot Charles Nungesser.

Above: François Coli was a skilled navigator.

THE WHITE BIRD

Charles Nungesser was France's ace of the air. Known as the "Knight of Death," he was a famous World War I fighter pilot, a barnstormer, and a stunt flier. François Coli was also a World War I combat aviator. Although he was wounded and lost his right eye, he continued to fly, and became known as "The One-Eyed Devil." In 1919, Coli set a distance record crossing the Mediterranean Sea. In 1927, Nungesser and Coli, two of the most experienced fliers in the world, would ultimately become men of mystery—lost forever while challenging aviation's limits.

Charles Nungesser was just 17 years old when he first sat down at the controls of an airplane in 1909. The teen quickly became a skilled pilot, growing more daring and reckless with every takeoff. When World War I broke out, he entered the French military. Brave and foolhardy, he became a fighter pilot in 1916. His silver Nieuport 17 plane was decorated with his insignia: a black heart, skull and crossbones, and a coffin with candles. Although he suffered several serious crashes and wounds, he survived the war, racking up 43 official air victories and becoming one of France's most famous pilots.

Above: French pilots Charles Nungesser and François Coli stand before the *White Bird*. Nungesser's black heart insignia is a sad symbol of these experienced pilots' last flight.

Above: Planning to land in New York Harbor, Nungesser and Coli ejected the *White Bird's* landing gear to cut down on weight. The landing gear now resides in France's Musée de l'Air et de l'Espace (Museum of Air and Space) at Le Bourget Airport.

After the war, Nungesser continued flying. He taught, performed in air shows, and became a stunt flier in American movies. However, he missed the excitement he'd had as a famous flying ace. In 1927, he found the challenge he needed.

Raymond Orteig, a wealthy New York City hotel owner, offered a $25,000 prize to the first plane to make a nonstop flight between New York City and Paris, France. Nungesser thought he could do it. He partnered with François Coli, who was an expert at navigating by the sun and stars. Planning carefully, they chose to fly a specially built, single-engine Levasseur PL8 biplane with an open cockpit. Named the *l'Oiseau Blanc*, or *White Bird*, Nungesser had the plane decorated with the blue, white, and red colors of France's flag, as well as his own well-known black heart insignia. The *White Bird* had a watertight fuselage that could float. The two men planned to eject their landing gear and land in New York Harbor after crossing the Atlantic Ocean.

On May 8, 1927, Nungesser and Coli rolled down the runway at Le Bourget Airfield, near Paris, France. Heavily overloaded with fuel for the long 40-hour Atlantic Ocean crossing, the *White Bird* had a difficult time lifting off. But the skilled Nungesser finally coaxed the Levasseur into the air. The plane did not have a radio, since the two men felt the device was too heavy and unreliable. No final words were heard as Nungesser and Coli flew off into adventure, tragedy, and mystery.

The *White Bird* was officially last seen off the coast of Ireland by a British naval officer, who recorded an entry in his logbook. Unofficially, witnesses in Newfoundland and Maine claimed to have seen or heard the plane the next day. People waited in New York, expecting to celebrate with the two brave Frenchmen. But Nungesser and Coli never arrived. An international search was conducted, but no trace of the plane or the pilots were ever found.

Above: Charles Lindbergh, 12 days after Nungesser and Coli's attempt to cross the Atlantic, made the flight from New York to France. Lindbergh visited Nungesser's mother, offering his sympathy and saying that her son's goal (France to New York) had been more difficult than his.

Charles Lindbergh, the man who 12 days later flew from New York to France, said that Nungesser and Coli "vanished like midnight ghosts." For more than 80 years, people have continued looking for answers to the pair's disappearance.

Some people thought the plane might have hit heavy headwinds and run out of fuel, causing the fliers to ditch in the Atlantic Ocean. Others wonder if Nungesser and Coli encountered a serious storm that brought them down over water. Without a radio, there would be no way for them to signal for help.

Some clues have led people to the Canadian province of Newfoundland. One theory is called the "plane in the pond." In 1927, 48-year-old Nicholas McGrath of Patrick's Cove, Newfoundland, was out trapping near Gull Pond, a remote area of rocks, bogs, shallow lakes, and scrub.

He heard three explosions, one after the other, but did not know what made these loud noises. The following year, McGrath was out hunting in the same area and found pieces of metal on the ground and in the rocks. He believed that it must have been airplane wreckage, linking it to the explosions he'd heard the previous year.

In the same area, over the course of many years, several people found pieces of what they thought was wreckage from the *White Bird*. However, none of the artifacts were ever positively identified to be from Nungesser and Coli's plane. TIGHAR (The International Group for Historic Aircraft Recovery) took a metal detector to Gull Pond in 1992. A lightweight piece of steel covered in gray blue paint was found. TIGHAR researched the artifact and the paint. In the *Illustrated Parts Catalog* for the Levasseur PL4 (from which the *White Bird* was developed), one paint color is listed: *gris blue* (gray blue). It's possible that this piece of metal was from the undercarriage of Nungesser and Coli's plane, although this is unconfirmed. It seems to show that an airplane crashed near Gull Pond. Was it really the *White Bird*? No one knows for sure.

Below: The Canadian province of Newfoundland is a beautiful but harsh island of rock, forest, lakes, and bogs. Some believe that Nungesser and Coli's plane, the *White Bird,* went down there.

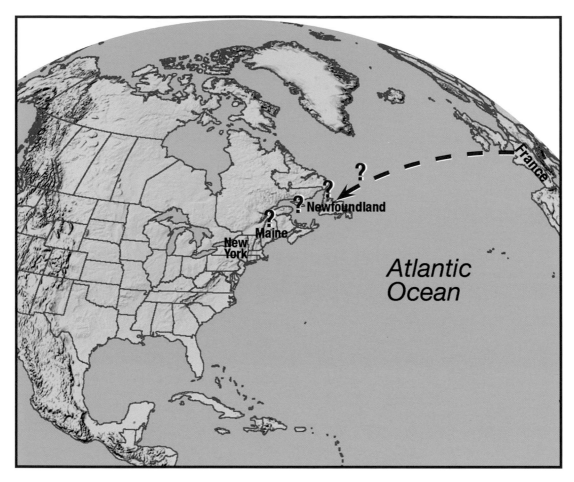

Above: A map showing the *White Bird*'s flight from France. Did the biplane crash in the Atlantic? Or possibly in Newfoundland or Maine?

Another story, from the state of Maine, places the *White Bird* only about 500 miles (805 km) from its New York destination. In 1980, freelance writer Gunnar Hansen did extensive research for a magazine article. Hansen talked to an elderly man, woodsman Anson Berry, who remembered hearing a plane crash 53 years ago. In 1927, Berry was out in the hills surrounding Round Lake, an area near the town of Machias, Maine. On May 9 of that year, late in the afternoon, Berry recalled being alone in the woods and hearing a plane fly overhead. It was a cloudy day, so he could only hear it. He remembered that the plane's engine didn't sound right. Not long after, he heard what he believed was the plane crashing in the distance. If the date and area are correct, the plane may have been the *White Bird*.

Building on Gunnar Hansen's research, TIGHAR and another archeological organization, NUMA® (National Underwater and Marine Agency), have both searched for the *White Bird* in Maine. Other stories, including someone finding an old rusted engine buried in the dirt (which has never been located again), keeps this area in the minds of searchers. However, the heavily wooded countryside, which is filled with bogs, makes it difficult to conduct a search. If the plane sank into the waters of a marsh or bog, it would likely be gone forever.

One thing that keeps this particular flight in the public eye is that if evidence is ever found that Nungesser and Coli made it to Maine, history would have to be rewritten. The French fliers, not Charles Lindbergh, would be the first people to cross the Atlantic Ocean. But for now, what happened to these brave pilots and their *White Bird* remains an unsolved mystery.

Above: Charles Lindbergh shakes hands with hotel-owner Raymond Orteig, collecting the $25,000 reward for being the first person to cross the Atlantic Ocean. But was Lindbergh first? Or was it really Nungesser (top) and Coli (bottom) in the *White Bird*?

MARY CELESTE

Above: Captain Benjamin Spooner Briggs commanded the *Mary Celeste*. In November 1872, he set sail with his wife, daughter, and a crew of seven. Although the ship was found, none of the people were ever seen again. *Below:* A stamp showing the *Marie Celeste*. Arthur Conan Doyle wrote a fictional story about a ship with this name. The name change from *Mary* to *Marie* has caused much confusion over time.

The *Mary Celeste* was a two-masted brigantine sailing ship found mysteriously abandoned in 1872. The fate of the crew and passengers of the "ghost ship" remains an unanswered mystery.

In 1872, the *Mary Celeste* was co-owned by three people. One of the owners was also the ship's commander, Captain Benjamin Spooner Briggs. Late in the year, Briggs was commissioned to transport a cargo of 1,701 barrels of industrial alcohol to Genoa, Italy. On November 7, the ship set sail from New York City with the experienced captain, a crew of seven, plus Sarah and Sophia Briggs, the captain's wife and two-year-old daughter. None of these people would ever be seen again.

On December 4, 1872, the captain and crew of the *Dei Gratia*, a British cargo ship, spotted the *Mary Celeste* floating aimlessly in the Atlantic Ocean. No signal flags were raised to indicate that the ship was in distress, but something was clearly wrong. After watching the ship for two hours, several crewmen from the *Dei Gratia* rowed over to the brigantine and boarded it. Although all the hatches were open and every inch of the ship was wet, the *Mary Celeste* was basically in good condition. However, not a soul was on board.

What happened to the 10 people sailing on this ghost ship? Speculation has ranged from the wild to the quite possible. Some guessed that aliens abducted everyone aboard the *Mary Celeste*. Others wondered if the crew had mutinied. Could pirates have attacked the ship?

No answers were found, and the strange story of the *Mary Celeste* might have faded away, except for an 1883 story by Scottish author Sir Arthur Conan Doyle, which brought attention back to the mysterious incident.

Mysteries of the Universe

The Marie Celeste

In December 1872 the Marie Celeste was found drifting off the coast of the Azores. The ship was abandoned, yet there was no hint of trouble in the log book, the cargo was safely stowed, and the galley and quarters were in order. For over a century the fate of the captain and crew of the Marie Celeste has been an intriguing mystery.

Maldives Rf25

The Marie Celeste

Left: An 1861 watercolor painting of the *Amazon*. The ship would later be known as the *Mary Celeste*. Still later, it was called a ghost ship.

Four years before he created his most famous character, Sherlock Holmes, Conan Doyle wrote "J. Habakuk Jephson's Statement," a story about a New England doctor who was the lone survivor of the *Marie Celeste*. (Conan Doyle's name change from *Mary* to *Marie* has caused much confusion over the years.) Combining fact and fiction, the story tells how the mysterious ship was taken over by a passenger and his cohorts, who murder everyone but the doctor, and sail the ship to Africa.

Conan Doyle's story gained great attention. Readers wondered if the crew of the recovery ship, the *Dei Gratia*, had killed everyone aboard the *Mary Celeste* in order to receive an insurance reward. What people forgot was that Conan Doyle's story was fictional. Although the young author was happy with his story's success and popularity, it brought unfair criticism to the captain and crew of the *Dei Gratia*. The facts were that the *Mary Celeste* was abandoned and its cargo was nearly intact. If the crew of the *Dei Gratia* had murdered those aboard, they probably would have stolen the cargo and taken the ship. Instead, they sailed the ship back to port and reported the strange situation to authorities. So what really happened to the people on the *Mary Celeste*?

No one knows exactly what happened to those aboard the *Mary Celeste*, but some guesses have been made. When the ship was boarded, it was wet, but still seaworthy. There was enough food and drinking water for six months. The captain's logbook was still aboard, but there were no hints of any problems. The cargo was still in the ship's hold, although it was later discovered that nine of the industrial alcohol barrels had leaked out their contents.

Besides the people, several important items were missing. The only lifeboat was gone. It appeared to have been launched, not broken away and lost. Several navigation instruments were missing, as were the ship's papers. Where did they go?

The most logical explanation is that the nine barrels leaking alcohol built up an explosive vapor in the hold. When the hold was opened, everyone smelled the strong fumes. Captain Briggs, believing that an explosion could happen at any moment, would have loaded everyone into the lifeboat. The lifeboat was supposed to remain tied to the ship, trailing behind at a safe distance. As soon as the open hatches and clean air cleared away the dangerous vapors, they would reel themselves back to the ship and climb aboard. However, clearly something did not go as planned. Most likely, the rope towing the lifeboat became untied. The crew and passengers would have been left to float helplessly in the ocean, as the *Mary Celeste* sailed away unmanned. Without fresh water, the people stranded in the lifeboat would have lasted only a few days.

Still, no bodies were ever found, which led to more speculation about the ship's ultimate fate. Other ideas include the ship encountering a waterspout or a seaquake, which would make it appear that the *Mary Celeste* was sinking, causing everyone to abandon ship. Some people even think that aliens may have abducted everyone aboard the ghost ship.

After it was recovered and refurbished, the *Mary Celeste* sailed under other owners for another 12 years. Finally, the ship's last captain tried to sink it in order to collect insurance money. Even then, the ghost ship would not sink, remaining above water and preventing any payout to the owner. Eventually, the ship did sink to a watery grave. Its wreck may have been discovered near Haiti on August 9, 2001, although the results of scientific testing have been inconclusive.

The ghost ship may have been found, but the actual fate of the captain, crew, and passengers of the *Mary Celeste* remains an unsolved sea mystery more than a century later.

Above: A two-masted ship sails into the sunset. What became of the ill-fated passengers and crew of the *Mary Celeste*? It remains an unsolved mystery.

USS CYCLOPS

In March 1918, the 542-foot (165-m) ship USS *Cyclops* disappeared without a trace somewhere in the Atlantic Ocean, taking the lives of 306 crew and passengers with it. Not counting warfare casualties, the tragic incident represents the largest single loss of life in U.S. naval history.

In 1917, the United States entered World War I. The U.S. Navy commissioned many ships to join the fight against the German Empire, including the bulk cargo ship USS *Cyclops*. The ship's captain, George W. Worley, had worked at sea for many years. He joined the Naval Auxiliary as a lieutenant commander in charge of the *Cyclops*. The ship was outfitted to transport coal to refuel coal-burning ships. It also acted as a troop transport.

Above: Although an experienced seaman, George W. Worley was disliked as commander of the USS *Cyclops*.

Although Worley was an experienced merchant seaman, his abilities to command a Navy vessel came into question after a few months. Several of the officers and crew charged Worley with drunkenness. Worley defended himself in military court, stating that it was the nerve disease beriberi that often caused him to lose his balance. Also, the medicine he took to fight this disease made him smell as though he'd been drinking. To the crew's dismay, the Navy cleared him of the charges, and he soon returned to his command.

In the early months of 1918, the *Cyclops* was assigned to transport a full load of coal from Norfolk, Virginia, to Rio de Janeiro, Brazil, South America. This coal would be used to refuel the U.S. ships in that area.

Right: The USS *Cyclops* was a bulk cargo ship originally launched in May 1910. Seven years later, in May 1917, the ship was commissioned for use in World War I by the United States Navy.

It was a tense, miserable trip. Still bitter about his trial, Worley often swore at crew members. His skills as a navigator repeatedly came into question. As the ship departed from the naval yard in Norfolk, Virginia, Worley narrowly missed colliding with another ship. On the way to their first stopover in Bahia, Brazil, Worley argued with the ship's navigator about their location. Hours later, Worley realized his error and had to double-back. Reportedly, neither officers nor crewmen found him to be a worthy skipper.

The *Cyclops* finally reached Rio de Janeiro on January 28. Over the next few weeks, the coal was unloaded, and 10,800 tons (9,798 metric tons) of manganese ore, a mineral used to make steel, was loaded onto the ship. In addition, repairs were made on one of the ship's high-pressure engines, which had blown a cylinder. Finally, more than two weeks later, 73 sailors came aboard, hitching a ride to Baltimore, Maryland, the *Cyclops'* destination. They never made it.

Above: The fleet enters the harbor of Rio de Janeiro in 1908. Some years later, ships like these would be refueled with coal brought from the United States by the USS *Cyclops*.

Below: A German military submarine, or U-boat (undersea boat), surfaces during World War I. Some people believe that the USS *Cyclops* was sunk by a German vessel. However, later research of German military records showed no enemy ships in the area where the *Cyclops* went down.

With a full load of cargo, plus crew and off-duty sailors, the *Cyclops* departed from Rio de Janeiro on February 16, 1918. The ship made an unscheduled stop in Barbados, in the West Indies, on March 3. Worley gathered additional supplies, then departed the next day. On March 4, 1918, the *Cyclops* steamed away from Barbados, headed toward tragedy.

When no word came from the ship by March 13, a vast Navy search-and-rescue began, centering between Cuba and Puerto Rico. Not one piece of debris was ever found. On April 15, the Navy released the news that one of its ships was "overdue." But as the days and weeks passed, it was clear that the *Cyclops* had vanished. From Navy personnel to family members to reporters—everyone began to guess the ship's fate.

Many thought a German submarine had sunk the heavily loaded ship. Some wondered if Ltd. Cmdr. Worley was a German agent.

Did he stop in Barbados to get extra supplies for a much longer trip across the ocean? Was the ship now a part of the German fleet? Certainly, a ship full of manganese ore would have been a valuable prize for the German Empire. However, the *Cyclops* was never seen again, not even with German markings. What mysterious circumstances could have caused the ship to disappear completely? No SOS was ever sent. In fact, the last message received from the *Cyclops* stated, *"Weather Fair. All Well."*

Although America was at war, an extensive search of German records in later years all but ruled out the possibility that a German mine, U-boat, or ship sank the USS *Cyclops*. An official U.S. Navy statement read, "The disappearance of this ship has been one of the most baffling mysteries in the annals of the Navy, all attempts to locate her having proved unsuccessful." However, researchers into this disaster have drawn their own conclusions.

Above: Earnest R. Crammer, a member of the crew of the USS *Cyclops.* He was one of the 306 people lost along with the ship. Aside from warfare casualties, this was the single greatest loss of life in U.S. Navy history.

With the ship as heavily loaded as it was, some believe that a storm or rogue wave may have struck the ship. This would have resulted in a shifting of the ship's load of manganese ore. If the ship listed to one side in a storm, it wouldn't take long for it roll over and sink. Survivors of the wreck would not last long in the waters of the Atlantic Ocean.

Still, people wonder why an SOS was never sent. Did something happen to the ship's transmitter? Or was there some kind of mechanical malfunction to the ship itself? One engine was repaired before the *Cyclops* left Rio de Janeiro. Was the work done properly? Could the engine have exploded in the middle of the Atlantic? Since no wreckage has ever been found of the *Cyclops*, that question may never be answered. As President Woodrow Wilson said at the time, "Only God and the sea know what happened." Even today, we can only make guesses about the *Cyclops*'s mysterious fate, and the fate of the 306 lost souls carried to their doom.

GLOSSARY

ARTIFACTS
Objects made or owned by a person or group of people. Often of historical interest, artifacts can be something worn, like clothing or jewelry, or something used, such as dishes or tools, or something created by a culture, such as art.

BIPLANE
A plane that has two sets of wings, one on top of the other. This was a common design of airplanes in World War I.

DAVY JONES' LOCKER
A centuries-old phrase of unknown origin meaning "the bottom of the ocean."

INSIGNIA
A badge, distinguishing mark, or decoration. In the military, an insignia may show a person's rank, membership, or nationality. An insignia may also be a special mark or logo. For example, Charles Nungesser had an insignia on his plane that incorporated a black heart, skull and crossbones, and a coffin with candles.

INTERNATIONAL DATE LINE
An imaginary line on the earth that shows where the end of one day and the beginning of the next come together. The Date Line runs vertically through the Pacific Ocean, from the top of the world to the bottom, mainly along the meridian of 180 degrees longitude, zigzagging in places so it goes through no land except Antarctica. Places on opposite sides of the line, although only a short distance from each other, are almost 24 hours apart. For example, when it is 7:00 a.m. Friday morning in New Guinea, it is 5:00 a.m. Thursday morning in Howland Island. This is because the globe is divided into time zones that total 24 hours.

NAVIGATOR
A person in charge of plotting the direction of ships, planes, or other forms of transportation. Historically, navigators used the sun and stars to find their way. As time passed, maps and special instruments were used. Today, many people navigate using GPS, the Global Positioning System, which uses orbiting satellites to pinpoint locations.

SONAR

A method of finding something submerged in water. A sonar device sends out sound waves and measures the time it takes for the echoes to return. The word comes from the phrase **so**und **na**vigation **r**anging.

THEORY

An idea or group of ideas that explains something. A theory is usually based on taking what is known about something—the facts—and combining them into a logical idea.

WORLD WAR I

A war that was fought in Europe from 1914 to 1918, involving countries around the world. Great Britain, France, Russia, and Italy (the Allies) opposed the Central Powers (Germany, Austria-Hungary, Turkey, and Bulgaria). The United States entered the war in April 1917 on the side of the Allies.

Right: In 1937, Amelia Earhart's disappearance brought about one of the biggest search-and-rescue missions in history. Over 70 years later, the search continues.

INDEX